HIDDEN
DEPTHS
a novel by Ian Strachan

CHAPTER 1

Dear Whoever-you-are,

Welcome to this house. I was very sorry to leave it because we loved living here so much and I bet you're thrilled to be here now!

Nicky broke off from reading the letter to let out a loud agonized groan. She'd found the note waiting on the doormat of their new house, addressed to "The Youngest New Occupant".

Thrilled was the very last thing she was, Nicky thought, as she gazed gloomily round her strange new bedroom. With no curtains at the windows and none of her colourful posters up on the walls yet, it looked so drab. Miserable, angry, upset, disappointed, yes – but definitely not thrilled!

Nicky wished she was back in her old, familiar room.

Oh, she thought, if only Dad could have been a *normal* kind of vicar. Why had he insisted on raising money for the restoration fund by doing a sponsored abseil down their old church tower? Although most of the village who had turned up had enjoyed the event, some of the older people had been so offended that they had written letters to complain to his boss, the bishop.

Nicky's father had been very gloomy when he returned from his meeting with the bishop.

"He thinks I'd be better suited to somewhere newer and more challenging. So he's sending us to Barnby New Town."

Nicky couldn't believe what her father was saying! For the fourth time in her life she was to be uprooted, losing her friends and having to start all over again at a new school. Nicky was sick of having to pack up and move on. She wanted to belong somewhere, instead of constantly drifting.

But what she really wanted was to stay in that house, way out in the country, where she was free to explore, climb trees, take home jars of frog spawn and help bring the cows up to the nearby farm for milking. It was a life which suited Nicky perfectly.

To make matters worse, the move had finally come during the summer holidays when Nicky should have been spending all her days with the Simpson children, riding Pickles, one of their ponies.

All her life Nicky had longed for a pony of her own, but of course Mum and Dad couldn't afford one. Then, just when she'd finally made friends with a family who had more horses than children, she'd been forced to move again.

This meant that instead of spending the whole day on Pickles, Nicky had wasted it, either sitting on packing cases trying to keep out of everyone's way, or handing out hundreds of mugs of thick brown tea to the removal men.

Finally, when everything was loaded up, Mum had set off on the back of Dad's motor bike, leaving Nicky to face the journey to their new home sandwiched between the men in the tiny cab of the removal van.

Being so cramped had brought back all Nicky's horrors about being trapped in confined spaces. Normally the bravest of people, whenever she was in a lift Nicky was secretly terrified. Common sense told her that nothing could go wrong, but she was convinced that the doors would never open again, all the air would be used up and she would die slowly of suffocation.

During the journey Nicky had tried to take her mind off her problems by looking out of the cab window, but entering Barnby had only made matters worse.

Instead of the rolling, open countryside which Nicky was used to, with a few cottages dotted about, the van threaded its way through a maze of tightly packed houses and blocks of flats. There were no fields, only handkerchief-sized gardens. No cows or horses, just the odd cat or dog, and the only trees had been so recently planted that they looked more like witches' broomsticks.

Barnby was a sprawling, brand-new town, built on what had once been countryside. It had swallowed up several tiny villages and only a handful of old buildings had survived, including Dad's church and their new vicarage.

The vicarage, outside which the removal van parked, had grown and changed over a long period of time. The oldest part was of grey granite and Nicky thought the up-and-down stones running round the edge of its flat roof made it look like the tower of a small castle.

The rest had been built and rebuilt over the years, although it was difficult to see the joins because the whole house was almost smothered with ivy. Its gnarled branches crawled across the walls like the tentacles of a giant octopus, eating into the mortar and choking up the gutters. Boughs hung down over the windows like drooping, sleepy green eyelids, keeping out most of the light.

As Nicky discovered when she stepped inside, the house was made up of huge, gloomy, draughty rooms which all smelt heavily of mould.

When the removal men had gone, and Nicky and her parents were eating a picnic meal in the ancient kitchen, Dad said cheerfully, "The church and the stone part of the house date back to the seventeenth century."

"Yes, Dan," Mum said, "and so does the heating system."

But Dad, who was never easily put off by the practical side of life when he faced a new challenge, added, "There's supposed to be a Priest's Hole hidden somewhere in the house."

"What's a Priest's Hole?" Nicky asked.

"It's where your dad will have to hide," Mum said grimly, "if he doesn't help get things straightened out! And Nicky, you ought to go and make a start on your room."

Sitting on her unmade bed, the bare floorboards almost hidden under a mixture of suitcases, cardboard boxes and overflowing tea-chests, Nicky longed to be back in her old home. That was when she remembered the note and started to read it.

"Oh, yes!" Nicky said bitterly. "You bet I'm thrilled to be in this dump!"

She was about to screw up the piece of paper, when she caught sight of the next sentence.

I'm sure it'll feel strange at first; it did for me, too, but there are good things around here and I'd hate you to miss any of them.

Some are secrets only I know, but I'm not going to just tell them to you. Instead, I've laid out a sort of trail for you to follow, with clues to solve along the way. It's a kind of challenge. Of course, you may think this is stupid...

"Too right," Nicky muttered.

... or you might just decide you can't be bothered. But in case you intend to take up my challenge, the floor-board in front of the window in the back bedroom – the one I expect you'll be given – lifts out and it's hollow underneath. That's where I kept all my secret things, and I've left the first clue in there.

If you decide this is the last of my letters you'll read, I'll say goodbye, but I still hope you enjoy the house as much as I did.

Signed: Your secret friend.
P.S. I really hope you take up the challenge!

"What rubbish!" Nicky growled, tossing the screwed-up note into the empty fireplace. "Kid's stuff! It's bad enough being in this horrid house at all, without playing stupid games."

Mum, who happened to be passing, poked her head through the open doorway. "What did you say, dear?"

"Nothing," Nicky mumbled.

Glancing at the mess, Mum said crossly, "You haven't done a thing in here yet! You'd better get the curtains hung and the bed made, at least, or you'll have nowhere to sleep tonight. I can't be expected to do everything."

Nicky was fiddling with the hooks on the first curtain, when she felt the floorboard rock slightly beneath her foot. Determined to ignore it, she hissed, "Clues!" and carried on fixing the curtain.

And yet, even when she had moved away and started making up her bed, the loose board and what might lie beneath it still tugged at a corner of her mind and she couldn't stop herself from glancing across at it.

Finally, while she was struggling to stuff her pillow into its case, Nicky could bear it no longer.

"It isn't that I really care, it's only curiosity," she said to herself. "But it's going to be difficult enough to get to sleep tonight, in a strange room, and I'll never make it until I know what's hidden under there!"

Tossing aside the pillow, Nicky marched across the room and knelt in front of the window. She felt around the crack of the loose board and gently prised it out with her fingernails.

In the gap between the rough wooden joists lay a small gold envelope. Nicky tore it open.

Dear Whoever,

Congratulations!

I'm really glad you decided to follow the trail. You've made the right decision, and I promise you won't be sorry. To give you an easy start, I've put the next clue in the hollow oak at the bottom of the garden, the one you can see from this window. Climb up inside and you'll find a biscuit tin waiting for you at the top.

Good luck!

Nicky drew back the curtains, but she'd left it too late, and the garden was in total darkness. "Just my luck!" she said, gloomily throwing the note aside.

CHAPTER 2

Having dreamed all night about riding Pickles, Nicky woke with no intention of following up the silly clue she had found.

But the moment she drew back the curtains, Nicky couldn't help seeing the huge old oak tree at the far end of the overgrown, walled back garden.

The temptation proved too great to resist. She quickly dressed in the previous day's green sweater and black jeans, ran her fingers through her short, jet-black, tangled curls and then hopscotched her way out, over the unopened boxes.

From her bedroom window the tree had seemed quite close to the house, but what had once been a vegetable garden was now head-high in weeds. Banks of nettles, cow parsley and dock had been tightly laced together by countless strands of burdock, bindweed and vicious sprawling brambles, until it formed a solid, green wall.

Nicky found a sturdy stick and, feeling like an explorer hacking her way through the jungle, began beating a path through the thicket. Several times during the struggle, as her hands and face got scratched and stung, Nicky grumbled, "This had better be worth it!"

She managed eventually to reach the foot of the oak. Round the back, in the base of the trunk, she found a hole like a low archway. Ducking inside, by the dim light, Nicky could see that most of the centre had rotted away, leaving a hollow running right through to a tiny patch of daylight at the top.

"But how do I get up there, to where the tin is?"

In the gloom, Nicky felt round carefully for some kind of handhold. Apart from the fact that this felt like the smallest lift she'd ever been in, she hated creepy-crawlies. She shuddered at even the thought of accidentally touching a woodlouse, or having a long-legged spider drop down into her hair.

Fortunately, she quickly found a very large nail sticking out from the inside of the tree and, as her eyes grew more accustomed to the light, she glanced up to see a whole series of nails, knocked in at regular intervals. "Almost like a ladder!"

Nicky heaved herself up on to the first nail and, holding on to the next, slowly began to climb. The closer she got to the light at the top, the tighter fit it became, but at least she was climbing towards the light and air.

Even so, she was relieved to haul herself out of the hole like a cork out of a bottle, especially when she found herself in a perfect lookout post. The best part was that, because of the screen of leaves, she could see without being seen. In fact, when the breeze blew, causing the branches to sway, Nicky could easily believe she was perched in the crows-nest of an old-fashioned sailing ship.

Nor was the view limited to Nicky's house and garden. The church had been built on a hill and the whole town lay spread out to her right, like the layout for a model train set.

Closer to home, on the left, Nicky looked down directly into another garden. Set at right angles to theirs, it had neat rows of vegetables, a fruit cage and a small orchard down the far side. From behind it peeped an old, white-walled cottage, with criss-cross leaded windows.

Nicky was wondering who lived there when she could have sworn she saw the face of someone watching her from behind the fruit cage. But, before she could get a proper look, the figure ducked down and although she waited, the face didn't appear again.

As Nicky sat on the branch, her feet dangling into the hollow, she spotted a red tartan short-bread tin, nestling in a hollowed-out knot-hole. Tearing off the sticky tape which had been used to keep out the damp, she opened the lid.

Apart from a note, there were several other things in the tin, including a piece of white card with lots of small holes cut through it, a piece of string with some knots along its length, and a rusty old iron key. Nicky unfolded the note.

Dear Whoever,

Welcome to the tree! This was where I always used to come to think, or when I simply wanted to get out of everyone's way. No grown-up will ever find you here. Some of the bits and pieces I have put in the tin may not make much sense to you at the moment, but you'll need them further along the trail. While I am very happy to share my secrets with you, there are things some grown-ups might kick up a fuss about. You know what they can be like! So just in case they happen to find one of my notes before you do, I thought it would be better if I wrote in different codes from now on. Grown-ups can be a bit thick, but they might manage to crack one. By the way, while you are still up here, count the windows along the top floor at the oldest end of the house and ask yourself this question:

how can 6 = 5?

Nicky obediently looked up at the top floor of the house and counted. There were six windows, one little more than a slit in the stonework, but she didn't understand the rest of the sum.

Think about that, but now back to the trail. The next clue is waiting for you when you find an angel called Rover. You need some local knowledge, and a visit to the library would help. On the way, if you haven't already got one, buy a torch. You'll need it later.

Good luck.

CHAPTER 3

Judging by the map of Barnby, which Nicky's mother had lent her when she'd asked where the library was, she must be half-way there, but it didn't feel like it.

"I hate dead straight roads, when you can see where you're going right from the very beginning," Nicky grumbled to herself. "It always seems to make it take twice as long to get anywhere. I'd much rather have our old, twisty country lanes."

The real problem was that around their old home Nicky was used to seeing familiar faces along the way and being able to stop for a chat, which made any journey seem shorter. In Barnby, everyone was a stranger to Nicky.

But the huge, bright library was a big improvement on the mobile library which visited Nicky's old village, and only parked by the village hall for fifteen minutes once a week. There were so many shelves that Nicky decided to ask for help with finding a local history book.

"I'm sorry," the librarian said, shaking her head, "but Barnby New Town hasn't been here long enough for anyone to write a book about it. Was there something special you wanted to know?"

Feeling a little silly, Nicky said, "Yes, I need to know about an angel called Rover."

To Nicky's surprise, the librarian smiled, "Oh, that's different. Here's a free leaflet, written by the Historical Society, about Old Barnby. I think you'll find what you need in there."

Nicky sat down at a table and began to read. There was a whole side on the history of the church, including a rather curious piece about a plate being missing since the seventeenth century. Nicky couldn't see what all the fuss was about, until she realized that the writer was talking about a paten, or communion plate, made of solid silver. Some of Oliver Cromwell's men were believed to have stolen the plate after they had laid siege to the church and vicarage during the Civil War. There was also a mention of the Priest's Hole.

Though no trace has ever been found of such a place, many still believe a Priest's Hole, or hiding place, does exist in the oldest part of the vicarage.

There was a rather gory story in the leaflet about a young boy being shot by one of Cromwell's men. During the siege, the twelve year old boy had been hanging out of an upstairs window shouting, "I'm for the King!" when one of Cromwell's Roundheads shot him and he died on the landing. Nicky couldn't resist a slight shiver as she read:

> **Superstition claims a bloodstain, which nobody has ever been able to remove, is still to be found on one of the upper landings of the house. It is said that the boy's tormented ghost has occasionally been seen.**

"Gosh!"

There were several paragraphs about some of the old buildings which had been knocked down to make way for the New Town, and a small pen and ink drawing of the front of Shepherd's Cottage, which Nicky recognized as being the one she had seen from the hollow tree.

"But what about the angel called Rover?"

She was almost at the end of the leaflet and was about to give up, when she spotted a paragraph headed:

Rover the faithful friend...

A Barnby man had good reason to be more than usually grateful to his dog. One winter's night in 1863, Mr Wendover of Squire's Edge Farm was walking back with his dog, Rover, from Indleberry, a distance of some eight miles. It was already dark when they set out, but soon they were caught up in a severe blizzard and, having lost all sense of direction in the snowstorm, they missed their way. Unbeknown to Mr Wendover, brickmakers had recently been at work in the area, extracting clay, and he fell into one of the marl holes which had been concealed by a snow drift. In falling, he struck his head such a dreadful blow that he was rendered unconscious.

Next day, when neither dog nor man had returned, Mrs Wendover organized a search party, but they found no trace of either. Having almost given up hope, they were about to turn for home when, some way off, they heard a dog howling. Struggling through deep snow, they found Rover lying across his master's body, keeping him warm and at the same time preventing the drift from burying them.

Thanks to Rover, Mr Wendover was rescued and restored to sufficiently good health to live into his nineties. But he never forgot the debt he owed his dog and when Rover finally died, aged fifteen, Mr Wendover asked permission for the dog to be buried in the churchyard. When this was refused, Mr Wendover laid the dog to rest in his own garden beside a yew tree and marked the grave with the statue of an angel.

"The angel called Rover!" Nicky cried out loud.

The librarian, who was passing with an armful of returned books, smiled. "You found what you were looking for, then?"

"Well, yes and no," Nicky said as she pored over her street map. "I know about the angel now, but where in Barnby is Squire's Edge Farm?"

"As a matter of fact, you're more or less sitting where the farmhouse used to be."

"Oh!" Nicky's face fell.

"But look at your map," the librarian pointed, "and see what's behind this building."

Nicky beamed. "Squire's Park!"

"Named after the farm because part of the park was once the old farm's garden."

"And is the statue still there?"

"Oh, yes."

"Thanks," Nicky said, as she jumped up and set off for the door. Suddenly she paused and turned back. "How will I know where to look?"

"Easy," the librarian said, "just look for the biggest, oldest tree in the park and the angel is almost underneath it."

Nicky's eyes widened. "The same tree?"

"Oh, yes. It's so old that people once made bows and arrows from its branches."

Nicky had no trouble finding the vast, sprawling, old yew tree and there, beneath it, standing on a marble plinth, was the white alabaster figure of an angel with tiny wings on the plinth, equally worn by time, was an inscription in old-fashioned writing.

Here lie the remains of Rover
who passed away in the year
MDCCCLXXVI

There never was a cleverer, more
useful, or faithful friend.
Gone ahead to be reunited some
time in the great tomorrow.

Clem Wendover

Expecting to find the clue on a note, as she had before, Nicky searched round the statue, but found nothing. She was still busy peering round the statue, when a hand suddenly dropped on her shoulder, grabbed a handful of sweater and hauled her up by it.

Nicky found herself looking into the red, angry face of an old man with white hair, who demanded, "Are you responsible for that?"

Nicky, puzzled but also very frightened, stammered, "I don't know what you mean."

But the old man wasn't listening. "You young people are all hooligans."

"But I haven't done anything," she protested. "I was looking..."

The old man shook his head. "Stands here unharmed for over a hundred years and then you have to come along and scribble all over it!"

Nicky hadn't the slightest idea what the man was talking about. "All over what?"

"If that's what you call graffiti, you can keep it! the man declared, pointing a finger at the statue. "You should be ashamed."

And then, before Nicky could say anything, the man suddenly released her and shouted, "I'm going for the police. You ought to be locked up, the lot of you."

As the man marched off across the park, Nicky looked more closely at the statue, but could see nothing wrong with it. Then she noticed the inscription. It was as if a child had gone along underneath some of the letters with a red wax crayon leaving tiny, random marks.

"That old man might be a bit deaf," Nicky said, with admiration, "but he's certainly got terrific eyesight to spot those little marks. Still, if he thinks I made them and he really has gone to get the police, I suppose I ought to try and get rid of them."

She bent down and, after spitting on a tissue, rubbed at the first mark under the n of remains. It disappeared quite easily. So did the one under the e of Rover. The mark beneath the x in the date was tricky to get at, but the t was no trouble to clean off.

Nicky was about to rub away under the c in cleverer, when she stopped and thought back over the letters she'd already removed. "N. e. x. t." she said in astonishment. "It spells a word, but probably only by accident."

She ran her finger along the rest of the inscription.

There never was a cleverer, more useful or faithful friend.

Gone ahead to be reunited some time in the great tomorrow

Clem Wendover

"CL UEATH OME and then TOMORROW all in one word, but the middle bit, after NEXT, doesn't make much sense."

It wasn't until she'd put all the letters together in her head and jiggled them around, that she came up with the answer: "Next clue at home tomorrow."

"It was a kind of code," Nicky said, rubbing away the rest of the marks. She was pleased that she'd discovered the solution, but disappointed it didn't tell her more.

On the way home, Nicky remembered the advice about buying a torch, but she couldn't help wondering about the clue on the statue.

"Tomorrow is fine, but why doesn't it say where I'm supposed to look for the clue?"

CHAPTER 4

Nicky searched everywhere for the whole of the following day but found nothing which looked remotely like a clue, coded or otherwise.

"But then," she sighed, "if it's anything like the last clue, I could look until I go purple in the face and still not find it!"

Having been so reluctant to start out on the trail in the first place, she was surprised to find how much she missed having another clue to solve.

Always supposing it wasn't right under her nose.

But even if it was, it would have been difficult to find. In the short time since they'd arrived, Nicky's room had managed to get into a dreadful state. Although she hadn't done any serious unpacking, during searches for things she couldn't live without, like clothes and Sadly, her teddy bear, Nicky had plunged into boxes and cases, carelessly pulling things out which had been left strewn across the floor.

Nicky was on her hands and knees, searching through the jumble she'd created, in case she'd accidentally buried the promised clue, when her mother paused in the open doorway.

"Isn't it about time you unpacked properly?"

"Probably, but I'll need help shifting some of the heavier boxes."

"I'll give you a hand when I come back from the attic."

"What are you doing up there?"

Mum brandished a huge wrench. "Haven't you heard the terrible knocking in the water pipes? I'm going to fix the ball valve."

Nicky couldn't help thinking how lucky they were that her mother was such a practical person. Some of the ramshackle vicarages they'd lived in would have cost a fortune to repair but for Mum's handiwork. The only mechanical thing Dad understood was the internal-combustion engine but, whilst he could strip a four-stroke motor bike down to its frame and reassemble it in record time, he was useless around the house.

At lunch time, Nicky joined her mother in the kitchen to eat cheese and slices hacked from a still-warm loaf of home-made bread. "Nicky, have you been up in the old part of the house?"

"No, not yet."

"I didn't think so. Nor had I, not until this morning. But I found a curious mark on one of the floorboards on the second floor landing."

"What sort of mark?"

"Well," Mum looked puzzled, "it's a sort of reddish brown and looks as if it was made by something like tomato sauce or blackcurrant juice. The strange part is, it almost felt as if it was still damp."

Nicky frowned, and then remembered what she'd read in the pamphlet. "The bloodstain!"

"Bloodstain?" Mum looked baffled. "What bloodstain?" Nicky repeated the story, including the part about the ghost, but Mum wasn't very impressed. "I'm sorry, Nicky, but I simply don't believe in ghosts and I've got much more faith in bleach than reappearing bloodstains. I'll have another go at it when I've got time."

At that moment, Dad's motor bike scrunched to a halt in the gravel drive and he breezed in to join them.

Nicky always thought her father, dressed in his crash-helmet and leathers, looked nothing like a vicar. Yet as soon as he removed the helmet, his ready smile, sparkling blue eyes and curly, black hair gave him the appearance of an impish cherub.

"Nicky, could I borrow your ghetto-blaster and some cassettes?"

"Yes, but why? I thought you hated all pop music after the seventies."

"Too true, but tonight I'm reopening the Youth Club in the church hall."

"Don't they have any music of their own?"

"Yes, a stack of scratched singles, but the record player was stolen months ago, which was why the club closed."

"Couldn't you buy them one out of the parish funds?" Nicky asked.

Dad shook his head. "Only if one turned up in a jumble sale. I'm afraid this is a very poor parish."

Nicky was surprised. "But Barnby's such a huge place."

"True," Dad agreed, "but sadly, few of them come to church and those that do aren't very well off. So there's very little spare money."

"Then how do you expect to persuade people to come to the Youth Club?" Nicky wondered.

"Easy," said Dad, with one of his wicked smiles. "I put a poster up in the local caff saying that, for Youth Club members only, I would be running a motor cycle maintenance course. Word has spread like wildfire."

MOTOR CYCLE MAINTENANCE COURSE

at
Barnby Parish Church
Youth Club
on Fridays at 7.00pm

open to
Youth Club members only

Mum groaned. "And I suppose that means you want me to do hair and make-up again, to keep the girls occupied?"

"Your hints and tips are always so popular," said Dad.

"If they're thinking of marrying anyone like you," Mum observed, "they'd be much better off with a crash course on drain-clearing and decorating."

But Dad wasn't listening and his natural good humour had faded. "I only hope the church will be able to afford to keep the Youth Club going."

Having spent the rest of the day unpacking and, at the same time, continuing the unsuccessful search for the clue, Nicky was feeling pretty tired and fed-up by the time her parents returned from the Youth Club. Mum looked particularly pleased when she announced, "Your father's got ten people on his motor bike maintenance course and four of them were girls, who refused to have anything to do with make-up classes."

"Nicky, who do you know who's on holiday in Greece?" her mother asked, as she came in the following morning and threw back the curtains.

"Nobody, why?" Nicky said from the depths of her duvet...

"Because somebody's sent you a postcard with a picture of Mykonos on it."

Nicky crawled from under the covers and rubbed the sleep from her eyes. On the front of the postcard was a picture of a donkey beside a white-sailed windmill, and when Nicky turned it over she found a message in familiar handwriting.

Tom and me are kite flying.
Kate is yacht watching. On Friday
Celia longs for a ride into town,
unless other things happen. Can Kate
borrow Laurie's haversack?
Bob only misses his xylophone.

Having read the nonsense message, Nicky had no doubt that the clue she had been searching for had arrived and was obviously in code. She peered closely at it, to see if there were any marks under the letters as there had been on the angel's stone, but there were none.

But she did notice several other things. Though the picture was of Greece, the postage stamp was British and she was certain that the blurred post-mark said Barnby and bore yesterday's date. Did that mean the writer still lived in Barnby?

And there was one other thing, which she found particularly odd. Whilst the message was addressed to "Dear Whoever", as always, her own name was above the address, though written in a different coloured ink and in completely different handwriting, as if it had been added later.

But who had found out her name and added it to the postcard? Apart from the librarian and the angry old man in the park, she hadn't spoken to anyone outside the family since she'd arrived in Barnby. The idea that somebody had been spying on her without her knowing gave Nicky a very odd, uncomfortable feeling.

CHAPTER 5

For several days, Nicky struggled without success to find a solution to the code on the postcard. She could easily see it wasn't mirror writing, but she wondered if it might be a number code, where she only needed to read a letter at regular intervals, say every second, or maybe third one. But whichever number she chose, Nicky always ended up with worse nonsense than she started with.

Most of the time she was trying to crack the code, Nicky spent perched in the upper branches of the hollow tree, which had become one of her favourite places. Several times, while trying to discover the hidden secret of the postcard, her eyes slipped across to her own name which reminded her that someone was watching her.

Remembering that the first time she had climbed the hollow tree, she'd been convinced someone had been watching from the next door garden, she kept a good lookout. Although she continued to have an uneasy feeling she was being watched, no matter how quickly she swung round, next door's garden always seemed innocently empty. Yet Nicky was always convinced she'd noticed some slight movement, even if it was only the twitch of a branch, as if somebody had just dodged back out of sight. "But I suppose it might have been the wind."

Then, one afternoon, Nicky nearly fell out of her tree when her eye caught a flash of yellow clothing; somebody really was moving around among the apple trees. Nicky waited impatiently, but every time it looked as if the figure was about to move out into the open, it would go back into the trees.

"Why can't you show yourself," Nicky hissed, but when the figure finally walked out into the paddock, it turned out that the person she'd been watching so eagerly was only an old lady in a billowing yellow skirt. Certainly not the kind of person to be involved with secret codes.

With a sigh of disappointment, Nicky laid her head back on the branch. She was looking back towards her house when she remembered the sum she'd been set, about the windows along the top floor of the old house: 6=5.

"Maybe if I can't solve the code," she murmured, "I should try something else."

Before she left the tree, Nicky checked the windows again. Including the narrow slit, there were definitely six. She headed off to look at the windows from the inside.

Nicky had almost reached the first landing, when she suddenly stopped in mid-step, convinced she'd heard a curious noise. It seemed to be coming from higher up the stairs but as soon as she stopped, everywhere was quiet.

"Must be my imagination," Nicky said, and was about to move on when the noise suddenly began again. It was a soft scratching noise which was definitely coming from somewhere above her.

"I hope it isn't mice," she muttered to herself, "or, worse still, rats!"

There had been rats in the Simpsons' stables. She'd often heard them nibbling at the old oak beams and sometimes, while she was getting fresh hay for Pickles, one of the red-eyed, long-tailed creatures would startle her by diving out from under the bale she lifted.

Step by step, as Nicky cautiously moved up the stairs, the scratching, scraping sound grew louder and more persistent. Nicky no longer had any doubts, there was definitely something up there.

"Maybe I can frighten it away," she said, and stamped her foot loudly. The bang echoed round the bare walls like a gunshot.

"Who's that?" Nicky sighed with relief as she heard her mother's voice coming from further up the stairs.

"It's only me, Mum," she called back, and galloped up to find her mother on her knees with a scrubbing brush and a bucket of water.

"I thought that scratchy noise you were making with the scrubbing brush was a rat. What are you doing?"

Without looking up from her task, Mum replied, "It's that stain I told you about."

Nicky peered down at the faint reddish-brown stain which was shaped like a map of Australia. "It looks as if it's almost gone."

"That's what I keep thinking," Mum replied, sitting back on her haunches. "This is the third time I'* tried to get rid of it and although it fades a little eac time, I never really remove it altogether and the nex day it's back, as bad as ever."

"I told you it was the blood of the boy they shot

Mum smiled, but shook her head. "I think it's much more likely to be sap coming up out of the wood."

"But this is the oldest part of the house," Nicky insisted. "This staircase must have been here for hundreds of years. There surely can't still be any sap left in it."

"Always supposing," Mum pointed out, "that thi is the original wood; but whatever it is, I'm determined to get rid of it. Anyway, what are you doing up here?"

"Just exploring," Nicky said, innocently, but as s carried on upstairs her thoughts were very much on the stain and the possibility of meeting the boy's ghost.

The staircase opened on to a dimly lit, broad corridor with closed doors down either side. Having worked out which was the back of the house, the sic facing the tree, Nicky counted the heavy oak doors. There were six.

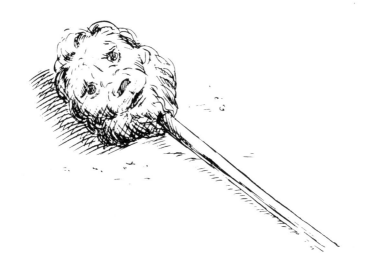

"Six equals five," Nicky murmured and, one by one, she lifted the latches, opened the heavy doors and peered inside each room.

They were all empty and much the same. The first five were quite small and each had a high win dow overlooking the garden. In some, patches of plaster were coming off the walls, or ceilings, and the bare floorboards were covered with a thick fur coat of dust, making it obvious that nobody had been inside any of them for ages.

But the sixth and final room was quite different. Unlike the others, though it was hardly bigger than a narrow corridor, it contained a huge, stone-surrounded fireplace. The fireplace was so big that Nicky could actually stand in it and it was obviously far too big for the room. On the hearth lay a poker with a handle shaped liked a lion's head

But, most important of all, as the door swung shut behind her, plunging her into darkness, Nicky immediately realized, it had no window. She quickly jammed the door open using the poker.

"Five rooms with windows and one without," Nicky said. "That's six windows minus five rooms, not six equals five. I need to find out what's happened to the sixth window, but there definitely isn't another room on this side of the house."

An idea suddenly struck her. "Maybe the missing window belongs to the Priest's Hole! Which means it must be hidden somewhere behind the fireplace wall."

Although she banged hard on all the walls, hoping to hear a hollow knock, they all sounded like totally solid stone.

She was busy knocking, when she froze. Just for an instant, she could have sworn she had heard a distant, answering knock. But when she tried it again, there was nothing. "Maybe it was just another echo," Nicky thought.

She continued to search the room and the corridor outside, but if the Priest's Hole was there, like hundreds of people before her, she couldn't find a way into it.

"But that still doesn't explain about the other window," Nicky said. Having been unable to find any possible explanation, she was about to leave when she looked at the floor.

The dust on all the other floors had been undisturbed. This one was covered in footprints. "Are all those really mine?" she wondered. "I suppose they must be. I'm the only one who's been up here and ghosts surely don't wear trainers."

She was on her way downstairs and had just passed the stain, which was looking damp, but very faint, when she heard another noise.

It sounded like footsteps following her down the stairs. Nicky stopped and so did they.

"Mum is that you again?"

There was no answer.

"Mum!" Nicky shouted anxiously. "I know it's you. Stop messing about."

Certain her mother was having a joke at her expense, Nicky turned and raced back up as fast as she could. She saw nothing until she reached the top landing, where the door of the room at the far end was slowly swinging shut.

Nicky ran down and threw it wide open. "Got you now, Mum!" she said and then stopped. The room was just as she had left it, completely empty and yet she could have sworn she felt a blast of cold air, coming from the direction of the fire-place...

"Have I been chasing the dead boy's ghost?" Nicky wondered with a sudden shiver. "But hang on a minute! I've never heard of a ghost using a door, they simply walk through them. You're imagining the whole thing," she told herself, crossly, "except for the bit about the missing window."

"There's something very odd about this house," Nicky said to her mother, when she found her back in the kitchen.

Mum smiled. "You mean apart from the plumbing, the blocked chimneys and the smell of mould?"

"It's the windows..."

"Yes," Mum agreed, "I haven't got round to cleaning those yet. Are you offering?"

"No Mum. But come outside."

Nicky led the way into the back garden and pointed up to the top floor. Without mentioning the trail she was on, or the noise she'd heard, Nicky explained about the number of rooms she could see and the fact that the slit window at the end didn't appear in any of the rooms.

"Oh, is that all," Mum laughed.

"But don't you see?" Nicky said excitedly, "I think it belongs to the Priest's Hole Dad mentioned."

Again Mum smiled, but this time she shook her head. "I'm sorry to disappoint you, Nicky, but that was probably bricked up in the days when the government taxed houses by the number of windows they had. There are two or three more bricked up round the side, hidden under the ivy. The only difference is, where the space was in the slit window, it's been painted to look as if the glass is still there."

Disappointed, Nicky went back upstairs, muttering, "I'm obviously no good at solving anything."

She did some more unpacking and stowing away, but she wasn't very enthusiastic. By now she'd got so used to moving house regularly, it hardly seemed worth doing a proper job. "We'll probably be packing it all up again in a few weeks' time," she grumbled. Then she realized how cross she'd really be this time, if she was forced to move before she'd finished following the trail!

Nicky was on her way downstairs, feeling quite peckish, when she noticed an envelope lying on the mat in the hall.

It had her name on the front but, when she opened it, there was nothing inside except for a blank sheet of paper.

"This gets worse!" Nicky said and headed for the kitchen. Intending to burn it later, she dropped the blank sheet of paper on top of the stove, and set about plundering the pantry.

After she'd eaten and was on her way out, she noticed the piece of paper, still sitting on top of the hot stove. "If I don't throw it away, Mum will only complain."

Nicky was just going to screw it up and toss it in the fire, when she noticed it was no longer blank. "Invisible ink!" she cried. "Why didn't I think of that!"

The heat of the stove had brought out the large words:

USE CARD WITH HOLES.

"Of course!" Nicky shouted and raced up to her room. She lifted the floorboard and, from her secret hiding place, took the piece of card with the holes punched in it, which had come from the biscuit tin. It was exactly the same size!

Tom and me are kite flying.
Kate is yacht watching. On Friday
Celia longs for a ride into town,
unless other things happen. Can Kate
borrow Laurie's haversack?
Bob only misses his xylophone.

She put the white card over the postcard's message. Suddenly, out of the jumble of meaningles words, as if by magic, a clear message appeared.

T	*a*		*k*	*e*	
K	*e*	*y*	*t*	*O*	
Cel	*l*		*a r*		
unl	*o*			*C*	*K*
b	*La*		*ck*		
Bo		*x*			

CHAPTER 6

A blast of ice-cold air rushed over Nicky as she opened the cellar door.

To avoid having to explain to her parents what she was up to in the cellar, Nicky had waited until they left for the Youth Club, which gave her two hours to unlock the secret of the black box. Nicky just hoped that, this time, it would be something more exciting than just another complicated clue, taking days to solve!

Finding no light, Nicky switched on her new torch. Its powerful beam pierced the darkness, revealing a flight of worn stone steps with a floor of granite slabs at the bottom.

Nicky shivered slightly. "This looks exactly the kind of place spiders love!"

Making certain she had the rusty old key for the box with her, Nicky carefully walked down the uneven steps. She'd been expecting to find something the size of a small coal cellar but, when she got to the bottom and shone her torch round, Nicky was surprised to find that the ceiling was nearly as high as in any of the rooms upstairs and brick arches appeared to open on to other rooms and corridors, which led off into darkness.

"Now to find the black box."

For a change, it turned out to be easy. The battered tin box was sitting in the corner opposite

the steps, under a stack of old magazines. She put i
the rusty old key and was delighted when she felt
the lock spring back. She raised the lid, and found a
ball of red wool with a note. Nicky heaved a sigh of
relief when she saw that the letter was written in
straightforward English.

Dear Whoever,

*OK, so you've got this far, but are
you brave enough to go on? It's
pretty spooky down here and to
reach the next clue, you'll have to go
somewhere much worse. Are you up
to it? I hope so, because it could get
pretty hairy from now on! If you give
up now, I'll understand, but if you
want to carry on it's simple enough.
From here, follow the white chalk
marks.*

Good luck.

*P.S. The ball of wool is to wind out
as you go, in case you are worried
about getting lost!*

"How can I possibly get lost in a cellar!" Nicky scoffed. She stuffed the ball of wool in her pocket and after finding the first chalk arrow, which pointed straight ahead, set off.

Fifteen minutes later, Nicky's head was spinning from weaving her way through the maze of corridors and rooms with only the echo of her own footsteps for company. Her torch beam had flashed across mouldy suitcases, mounds of discoloured newspapers and a huge, empty rack for wine-bottles, draped in a curtain of dusty cobwebs. She had climbed over half-walls into separate sections, wriggled through tiny gaps and gone round so many corners, she'd completely lost all sense of direction and was covered from head to foot in dust.

Suddenly, totally bewildered, she stopped. "I'm sure I've seen that rusty coal shovel before. I mean, how many rusty shovels can there be down here?"

Nicky squatted on her haunches and wondered what to do. "I could be going round and round in circles. Maybe I ought to rub out each mark as I go past it. Then I can't possibly use the same one twice."

Nicky was about to remove another mark when she suddenly realized the danger in what she was doing. She dropped her hand, horrified.

"If I rub out all the marks while I'm going this way, I might never be able to find my way back."

Suddenly the idea of unravelling the ball of wool didn't seem such a silly one after all.

But thinking about that brought back the story of an old Greek legend which they had done at school. In it, while going through an underground maze, somebody had unravelled string, but they'd met a huge angry monster with the body of a man and the head of a bull. The really gory bit, which Nicky had lapped up at the time but wished she hadn't remembered while she was alone in a cold, dark cellar, was that the monster lived on human flesh.

Down there, in the spooky tangle of rooms and corridors, she could easily imagine herself turning a corner and finding a human skeleton. From there it was only a short step to worrying about never getting out and becoming a skeleton herself.

Nicky shuddered, but then pulled herself together. "I'm being silly. The last person who lived here got out again, otherwise they couldn't have left me the note. And if they can get out, so can I. Still," she said, pulling the crushed ball of red wool from her pocket and firmly tying the loose end to the leather handle of an old trunk, "there's no point in taking stupid chances."

Letting the ball unroll as she walked, Nicky kept following the chalk marks, but just the thought of meeting a monster with the head of a bull made her much more wary about going round corners.

Nicky was busy trying to convince herself that there couldn't possibly be any kind of monster living down here, when something feathery and dry dragged across her face. She opened her mouth to scream and found herself trying to pick bits of dusty old cobweb off her tongue. Nicky clawed at strands which clung to her face and eyelashes, while her scalp tingled furiously as she imagined she could feel the long legs of the web's owner crawling slowly through her hair.

When she had calmed down, Nicky realized she had come to a dead end, facing an old wooden cupboard which had been built into the wall.

"I must have taken a wrong turning." When she checked back along the wool, the signs definitely indicated she had taken all the right turns. "But what now?"

Then, just poking out from a crack in the mortar between two bricks, low down near the floor, Nicky spotted the end of a carefully folded slip of paper.

Dear Whoever

You made it, good for you, but I must own up. For future use, there is a quick way here. If you look straight back, you should just be able to see the foot of the cellar steps.

Nicky shone the torch back up the narrow corridor and was furious to see that what the note said was true and to make matters worse, several strands of red wool criss-crossed pointlessly from one side to the other.

"Then why have I been wasting time, scaring myself to death and crawling round the entire universe?" Nicky demanded.

I wanted you to use my round-about route to see if you are really up to the next part of the trail, and because you've made it here, you must be.

The cupboard in front of you has a false back, slide it to the left and you'll find a hole in the wall. I found it once when the whole family was playing hide-and-seek. They never did find me and I never told anyone about it.

Once inside, you have a choice. I suggest you go up the stone steps which date back to when they had servants here. At the top, I promise you'll find the key to at least one of your problems and another coded clue. It's very dark and although the steps are stone, they're very narrow and crumbly so take great care.

Good hunting.

Without hesitating for a second, Nicky opened the cupboard door and ignored the warning squeal of its rusty hinges, which echoed eerily around the dark, empty cellar.

CHAPTER 7

At the back of the cupboard Nicky found a crack in the panel which she could just grip with the tips of her fingers.

"Here goes," she said softly. Nicky pulled and the entire panel slowly slid away, revealing a narrow stone platform. "Wow! It really is a secret passage," she said as she stepped through.

On her left, was little more than a gap which had been left in the stone wall. When Nicky poked her head through, it seemed that the floor dropped away steeply beneath a low, rough ceiling and in the distance she could hear dripping water.

From her right, a set of shallow stone steps rose round the first sharp bend of a spiral staircase.

Of the two, the hole looked by far the most interesting, but having glanced at her watch and realized there was only an hour before her parents came home, she decided to follow the advice of the note and go up the stairs.

She seemed to be climbing for ages. Her legs ached and she was starting to feel dizzy from going round and round all the time, while constantly having to watch where she put her feet on the uneven steps.

Suddenly she heard, from somewhere above her a strange knocking sound as though somebody was banging the wall with a big hammer.

"But, unless the Youth Club's packed up early," Nicky whispered, "I'm the only one at home..."

Several times, while Nicky held her breath and listened, the banging stopped, only to start up again, louder and more persistent than ever.

Nicky felt trapped. While the curious noise still vibrated through the walls of the building, she was frightened to go on. At the same time, she was afraid to return to the main part of the house, which she had left in semi-darkness. It was there that any intruder was most likely to be lurking.

Of the two alternatives, going on appeared the least dangerous and so, trying to shut out the noise, she carried on up the staircase.

A short while later, glancing upwards, Nicky was convinced that the stone wall up ahead was glowing slightly, almost as if a cold, ghostly light was seeping down the stairs towards her.

Nicky told herself, "You really are letting your imagination run wild." But when she briefly switched off the torch there was no doubt and, when she rounded the next bend, the explanation became obvious. Moonlight was pouring in through the slit window.

"So for once, Mum was wrong! That's why 6 = 5! Because the sixth window was hidden away on this staircase and I'm now on the top floor. And that's the problem the note said I'd solve."

She couldn't help feeling disappointed. All the way up, Nicky had been hoping she was about to discover the Priest's Hole but the way ahead was blocked by a solid stone wall.

However, when she flashed the light across the wall, up near the top, Nicky thought there seemed to be a narrow gap behind an overhang.

Hoping she might still be about to find the Priest's Hole, she scrambled up until she was lying in a slit which ran across the top of the wall, her back painfully pressed against the rough ceiling. Shining her torch down on the other side she saw, not the Priest's Hole, but the light reflecting off the surface of a brass poker with a lion's head handle!

"I'm looking down into the fireplace of the room at the end of the corridor. So this must be a secret way from the top to the bottom of the house."

Nicky had hardly uttered the words, when a shadow flitted across the fireplace. Believing she had finally met the ghost of the boy shot by Cromwell, Nicky was so startled that she almost fell off her risky perch and back down the staircase. But then she heard someone say,

"You're dead right."

Nicky's voice quavered when she asked, "Who's there?" Then she felt even more stupid as she added, "Are you a ghost?"

"No, I'm real enough," A girl of about Nicky's age, with short, blonde hair and a broad smile, ducked under the mantel and appeared in the fireplace. "Hi, Nicky, I'm Laura."

"But what are you doing in our house," Nicky demanded, "and how do you know my name?"

"Take it easy," Laura said. "You look very uncomfortable up there. Why don't you come down and join me and I'll explain everything."

While Laura switched on the room's main light, Nicky jumped down and they sat on the edge of the hearth. Laura started by producing a half-empty bottle of tomato sauce. "This is what I was doing, replacing the bloodstain on the landing."

Although she was still wary, Nicky couldn't suppress a smile. "No wonder Mum said it kept coming back!"

"Exactly."

"And was that you banging just now?"

"Banging?" For a second Laura frowned, until she realized what Nicky was talking about. "Oh, that! No, it was the water pipes. They've always done that but I've got used to it, I didn't even notice them tonight."

"Of course," Nicky said. "Mum tried to stop that happening, but it sounds so different..." Nicky had been about to mention the staircase but she wasn't sure whether to trust a girl who was playing tricks and so she settled for, "Sounded different tonight. But you still haven't explained how you got into the house."

"More or less the same way as you, up the stone staircase, but it nearly scared me to death when I heard you," Laura admitted. "I didn't think you would have solved that clue yet."

Nicky was astonished, "So you know all about the trail?" Laura nodded. "Is it you who has been setting the clues?"

"Oh no, that was all Richard's work. We were great friends until his parents moved. He unearthed all the secrets of the house and we shared them. When Richard had to leave, he didn't know who was coming to live here and didn't want to pass everything on to just anyone, in case they gave the all away. Which was why Richard set up the trail. He thought, if whoever came couldn't be bothered solve the clues, then they didn't deserve to know. You've done really well."

"But I still don't understand how you got into the house. You didn't come through the cellar."

"Haven't you collected the final clue? The one Richard left in the crack by the window?"

Nicky shook her head.

"Well, I may as well tell you. It's the last part of the trail, but easily the most exciting. You know the story about the Priest's Hole?"

Nicky's eyes widened eagerly. "Yes."

"Well, if there is one, Richard never managed to find it."

Nicky looked disappointed.

"But," said Laura, "there is an underground passage which we think was used by priests to escape from the house. It leads to Shepherd's Cottage, where I live."

"The house next door! Was it you watching me from the garden?"

"'Fraid so."

"But I only ever saw an old lady."

"That's Gran," Laura explained. "My Dad's in the RAF and he keeps getting posted all over the world. So my parents leave me with Gran. That way I don't have to keep swapping schools and stuff."

Nicky nodded sympathetically. "It isn't much fun moving round all the time."

"No," Laura said, "though it has been very quiet here since Richard left. He said that when new people came, I ought to keep coming through the tunnel and replacing the blood, just for fun."

"What's the tunnel like?"

"Dark, damp and because it's falling apart in places, very dangerous," Laura explained. "It was supposed to be the final challenge. Richard's terribly clever, and he set up a trip wire that would ring a bell in my room when you came through. That way I could open my end of the trap to meet you and welcome you as a full member of our secret society."

Although Nicky didn't much like the sound of the tunnel, she didn't want to look silly in the eyes her new friend and decided the sooner it was over with the better. "Can we go through it now?" Nicky suggested.

"Are you sure you want to?" Laura asked, and grinned when Nicky nodded. "OK then, come on."

They helped each other back over the wall. Laura pulled a torch from her pocket, but put the sauce bottle down on the top step. "I don't think I'l be needing this any more, so I think I'll leave it here."

Nicky looked puzzled. "Why?"

"Just suppose, a thousand years from now they knock the house down. They'll find a twentieth-century sauce bottle standing at the top of a sealed-off sixteenth-century staircase. That should give them something to think about!"

Nicky laughed. "Like a clue for another trail!"

"Which reminds me, here's Richard's last clue," Laura said, taking a slip of paper from a crack in the wall and handing it to Nicky.

This one contained no words at all, just line aft line of equally spaced letters. "I'd never have solved it," Nicky confessed.

"You cracked all the others, so I'm sure you would. Remember the piece of string with the knot in it, from Richard's biscuit box?"

Nicky looked blank. "Yes."

"If you lay that string under each line," Laura said, "the knots tell you which letters to use. It's another version of the red crayon dashes under the inscription on the angel."

"You knew about all the clues?"

Laura laughed. "Yes, but you've no idea how pleased I was, the day after you moved in, to see you appear in the hollow tree. Then I knew you'd taken up the challenge and eventually I'd be making a new friend."

"Did you send the message in invisible ink?"

"Yes, I wrote it in lemon juice."

"And did you write my name on the postcard?"

"That's right. Richard said not to post it until you'd solved the Rover puzzle, but you were so quick I didn't have time to find out your name."

"So how did you manage that in the end?"

Laura smiled. "I went to the re-opening of the Youth Club and asked your Mum."

"That reminds me," Nicky said, looking at her watch. "We'd better get going, or they'll be back and wondering where I've gone."

Together, they ran down the steps, pausing briefly at the bottom to close the cupboard door and the sliding panel before climbing through the narrow gap which led to the tunnel.

"It wouldn't do for them to stumble across that," Laura said. "You know what grown-ups are like. Gran knows nothing about the tunnel. If she found out, I'm sure she'd say it was too dangerous and get it filled in."

Nicky hadn't gone far, following Laura down the steep, low slope, when she began to wonder if Laura's grandmother might have a point!

In several places, pieces of the slimy stone sides had caved in, leaving patches of dank earth showing through. Further on, where a large section of roof had given way, they were forced to wriggle through a narrow gap between the ceiling and a pile of stone rubble.

Water dripped continually through cracks in the roof, where it had helped form tiny grey stalactites. There were also some curious growths of yellowy-brown fungus, oozing from between stones like frozen bubbles of curry-coloured bubblegum.

Nicky was beginning to wish she hadn't insisted on coming. The tunnel made her feel trapped and she was just wondering if she could summon up the courage to ask Laura if they might go back, when she suddenly heard a distant but strong rumbling noise.

Although it came from much further down the tunnel, Nicky felt the floor tremble beneath her feet. Rubbish, dislodged from between two roof stones, trickled out and ran straight down Nicky's neck. "What's making that awful noise?" she asked.

Laura, who was more used to the tunnel, was some way ahead. She happily called back over her shoulder, "Don't worry, it's only a big lorry using the road past our house."

In spite of Laura's explanation, Nicky started feeling flushed and it was becoming difficult to get her breath, all the usual warning signs of a panic attack. If only they could get out, she thought. She forced herself to ask, "How much further is it?"

"Not far," Laura called back, "we just go round..."

Laura's words were suddenly drowned by a loud roar, as an avalanche of stone and earth, shaken loose from the ceiling by the vibrations of the lorry, poured down.

Before she blacked out, Nicky heard a loud clunk, as something metal fell on her. After that the whole ceiling collapsed, completely burying her.

CHAPTER 8

Nicky came round feeling as if she was trying to swim upwards through thick porridge. She thought she had opened her eyes but everywhere was completely dark and there was a tremendous weight pressing down over her whole body, making it almost impossible to breathe. What air there was smelled old and used.

As if waking from a deep sleep, she vaguely remembered being in the tunnel and the roof falling in on her.

Nicky attempted to move her legs, but couldn't. Nor could she move the first arm she tried, but after a good deal of effort she managed to drag her second arm towards her face through slightly looser, wet soil. When it was almost there, she touched something she didn't understand at all. So far as she could tell in the dark, it was metal and round, rather like a dustbin lid. Probably part of the debris which had fallen on her while she was following Laura.

Laura! What had happened to her? Had she been buried too? Thinking the word "buried", brought Nicky completely to her senses. Everything was dreadfully clear. She had been buried alive.

A hot sweat of fear poured over her body. Nicky opened her mouth to scream for help, but it was instantly filled with soil and bits of stone, which coated her tongue and threatened to choke her.

She spat out what she could and tried to breathe only through her clogged nostrils. It was all her worst nightmares rolled into one and far worse than being trapped in a lift.

Nicky was convinced she was going to die,

buried alive. Images from her past – her parents and Pickles the pony, – drifted through her mind, but though she tried to cling on to them, they kept fading away.

Soft, gentle tears of hopelessness escaped from between her closed eyelids and trickled away into the mud daubed on her face.

Nicky had been sobbing for quite some time, when she remembered that the tunnel had been the final part of Richard's challenge. Suddenly she felt very cheated at getting this far, and even finding a new friend in Laura, only to lose everything. In a way it was the very worst kind of being moved on.

"But why should I? I'm not going to give in," she told herself fiercely, "at least not without a struggle." Maybe Laura wasn't trapped, or she'd already escaped and gone for help.

She tried to move her free hand backwards and forwards a little more, trying to gain a little space. At first it seemed hopeless but, little by little, she did gain more room.

Slowly, using her hand like a trowel, she started to dig the soil away. At first it ran back into the hole she'd made and she half wondered if it was really worth the effort.

"But anything's better than lying here, doing nothing!"

Again she started to move handfuls of earth away and this time, because she packed it down as hard as she could, as if she was making mud pies, it stayed put.

Because in the dark she had no way of knowing which way was out, Nicky concentrated on trying to free herself. The dustbin lid had obviously helped to protect her and might still be shielding her face from heavy objects. It had certainly provided a slight air-pocket, even though it smelled none too sweet. She decided it was best left, so she concentrated on freeing her other arm. With little breath and only able to make slight movements, it was hot, tiring work, but eventually Nicky's arm was free and she used it, under the lid, to clear some soil away from around her mouth. When she had removed the worst, Nicky started to shout for help, whilst at the same time carrying on with the job of trying to free as much of her body as possible.

Nicky had no idea how long she'd been unconscious, so hours seemed to have passed before suddenly the weight which had been pressing down on her seemed to be relaxing a little, the digging got slightly easier and Nicky believed she could hear muffled voices.

"Probably my imagination again," she thought. But she still took the deepest breath she could manage and shouted, "Help!"

Without warning, the lid was suddenly lifted off her face. Automatically she opened her eyes and then shut them again, blinded by the torchlight flashing in her face.

An unfamiliar voice cried out, "She's all right!"

Through half-closed eyelids Nicky found herself looking up at a red-faced lad. He wore a heavily chained and studded black leather jacket and a red and white bandana tied round his forehead, on which was tattooed BAZ. "Don't worry. We'll soon have you out of there, love."

"Thanks," Nicky said weakly, happy to let others do the work.

Two more bikers, together with Nicky's father, carefully climbed down into the pit and began to scoop the earth off her. Behind them, looking anxious, Nicky could see her mother, Laura and several other people from the Youth Club, who had all come to help.

"Nicky," Dad said, while he kept digging round her legs, "are you all right?"

"I will be," Nicky smiled, "once I'm out of here."

She was soon being lifted out of the hole and found she was emerging from the ruins of what had once been the neat and tidy Shepherd's Cottage vegetable patch.

But the thing she noticed most, after struggling to breathe the stale, rancid air underground, was the wonderful cold, clean smell of fresh air. As she stood

up, Nicky breathed it in so deeply it made her giddy.

"Take it easy," Mum said, slipping her arm round Nicky's shoulder. "You might have broken something."

Nicky cautiously moved both legs and then twisted her head back and forth. "Everything seems to be all right," she said, brushing mud off her sweater and jeans. "I think that dustbin lid thingy must have saved me from getting really hurt."

"Maybe you ought to keep it as a souvenir," Laura suggested. She picked up the metal object, brushed some dirt off and then looked at it more closely. "Do dustbin lids usually have writing on them?"

Without turning to look, Dad said, "Sometimes it says on them what council they belong to."

"This must be a foreign dustbin lid then," Laur suggested. "The writing round the edge is in Latin.

Dad turned round sharply. "May I see that?"

Once it had been cleaned by experts, Nicky's 'dustbin lid" went on exhibition in the church hall and hundreds of people travelled from all over the country, and abroad, to see what had turned out to be the missing solid silver plate.

"Richard will be really jealous," Laura had said to Nicky the next day, while they were sitting up in the hollow tree, "when I write and tell him how you recovered the buried treasure!"

"We!" Nicky insisted. "We found it. Let's face it, the plate wouldn't have been found at all, and neither would I, well, not alive, if you hadn't got out and gone to the Youth Club for help."

"So old Oliver Cromwell didn't steal the plate after all."

"Some clever priest must have hidden it in the secret tunnel and forgotten to recover it."

For a few moments they watched the workmen who were filling in the hole in the vegetable patch, left by the collapse and rescue.

"I'm glad," Nicky said, "that you didn't let on to your grandmother that the tunnel went right through to the vicarage, otherwise they'd have found out about the other secrets."

However, the girls struck a pact never to use the secret staircase unless they were together. Which wasn't a problem. From the day they met, Laura and Nicky were hardly ever apart.

The money raised from the exhibition made certain that the Youth Club kept going and in recognition of their part in the rescue, they also got a brand new music-centre with a stack of CDs, a complete workshop of tools for the motor bike classes and a state-of-the-art burglar alarm, so that nothing would be stolen from the church hall again. Reports of Nicky's rescue and the recovery of the plate appeared in all the papers.

One day the phone rang. It was Richard for Nicky, ringing from Dubai.

Only having read letters from him until then, Nicky found it odd talking to him. He was very nice and congratulated her on everything, but Nicky couldn't quite come to terms with the way he talked about the vicarage. He almost made it sound as if it was still his house, while Nicky was quite positive it was now her home.

Several weeks later, while Nicky and Laura were in Barnby New Town's shopping precinct, Nicky realized that, for the first time in her life, she was using the lift without any problem at all. Nicky had never told Laura how frightened she'd been in the tunnel, even before the roof fell in and she smiled quietly to herself.

But there was one rather odd thing.

It was months after the cave-in. Nicky and Laura were up in their favourite meeting place, the hollow tree, sharing a monster bag of crisps, when Nicky said, "I thought we'd agreed never to use the secret staircase alone."

Laura nodded.

"And," Nicky went on, "that you'd completely given up playing tricks with the tomato sauce bottle and the bloodstain on the landing?"

"I have," Laura replied.

"Well, I went up there last night and the stain was back again." Nicky's mouth dropped open for a second. "But if you didn't do it..." Nicky's voice trailed away.

The two friends stared at each other, wide-eyed with disbelief.

THE END